INSIDE OUT IN

ISTANBUL

Making Sense of the City

LISA MORROW

Inside Out In Istanbul: Making Sense of the City

Second Edition

Published by Lisa Morrow

Copyright © Lisa Morrow 2015

ISBN 978-1482063455

www.insideoutinistanbul.com

Cover design © Lisa Morrow 2015
Cover and back page photos © Kim Hewett 2001, 2004

This book is dedicated
to my darling Kim,
who gave me all the time I needed
to think and dream

Table of Contents

Acknowledgements

Many people have helped me realise my dream of publishing a collection of essays about Istanbul. In particular I want to mention my father Geoff Morrow who always listened to my stories about my life in Istanbul before his death in late 2013. I would also like to thank my best friend Sonay Koman for answering all my questions about Turkish life, even the awkward ones. Trevor Keeling kindly completed the layout of the cover. Lastly I want to say how much I appreciate the support of my husband Kim Hewett, who gives me all his encouragement and love.

Most of these stories originally appeared in a slightly different form on my blog www.insideoutinistanbul.com. Previous versions of the "Introduction" and "The People You Meet" were included in the first edition of *Inside Out In Istanbul*, released in 2013. "A Touch of Spice" was first published in *Lale: Magazine of the International Women of Istanbul*, Issue 5, May 2014.

Introduction

Turkey is a country that wrestles with the juxtaposition of tradition and modernity. These two disparate influences compete on a daily basis, and the foreigner, in the midst of such contrasts, is often left confused and bewildered. Of course, any country where you were not born, and do not share the same language or religion will be foreign and therefore strange, but Turkey also has an extraordinarily diverse population. Everyone you meet here will identify themselves as a Turk, but being a 'Turk' can mean many things. The smooth talking salesperson in a carpet shop or the stony-faced village woman who stares at you unremittingly for hours at a time on a long distance bus trip are both Turkish, but can come from any one of a multitude of backgrounds.

A Turk can be a person from a tiny mountain village cut off from larger towns for several months of the year, who has only ever seen foreigners on television. Some have never been further than the next town and never ridden on a bus larger than the village minibus. They may be from *İç Anadolu*, the harsh and arid interior of the country that breeds fierce, hardworking farmers. This area of the country is a popular destination for tourists keen to see the famed fairy chimneys of Cappadocia so locals dressed in traditional baggy pants and headscarves mingle with foreigners wearing shorts, in an at times uneasy harmony. Other Turks live along the Mediterranean coast and share more than a physical resemblance to the former Greek inhabitants and play host to millions of bikini clad Europeans every year. Yet other Turks live close to the borders of Iran and Syria and speak Turkish as their second or even third language. They rarely if ever see Western tourists, and what they know about the rest of the country and the world is what they glean from television, with its exaggerations and fallacies.

There are around eighty million people in Turkey today, and about twenty million* of them live in Istanbul. The city is home to Turks from all over the country, coming from north, south, east and west, bringing with them specific traditions and customs, prejudices and beliefs. With the rush to modernise that hit the country after the tumultuous decades leading up to the 1990s, more and more people have flocked to Istanbul, seeking greater opportunities and a better life. They live cheek by jowl

---

*although official figures estimate the population of Istanbul to be around fifteen million people, unofficially the real figure is thought to be closer to twenty million.

with the original inhabitants of Istanbul, a collection of peoples who evolved from the Ottoman Empire with its multicultural population consisting of Armenians, *Rum* or Turkish Greeks, *Çerkez* peoples from the Balkans, Russian exiles, Jews and more. For this reason, Istanbul is the showcase of Turkey, not because of its history, archaeology or other inanimate qualities, but because of its people.

In other cities of this size a huge number of people living in close proximity can lead to alienation and a certain lack of soul. Yet despite the enormous mass of people in the city, Istanbul is really just a series of interconnected villages. Just like any village in any part of Turkey, my Istanbul neighbours gossip and help or hinder one another, the local shopkeepers know who has money and marriages problems, the watermen, tailors and shoemakers pool information about new residents, and everyone knows about the foreigners in their street.

There are plenty of travel books about Turkey that lead you step-by-step through its many important sites. Whether you are fascinated by the history, architecture, religion or food, there is a book written to answer even the most obscure question. However there is little to introduce the curious to the seemingly mundane yet intriguing aspects of life in an Istanbul suburb. Beyond the cosmopolitan whirl of the European side of Istanbul seen by most tourists, tradition still plays an important role in everyday routines. Among the most well-known Turkish practices are taking off your shoes inside the house, fortune telling by reading coffee grinds and drinking tea, all conventions general to Turks across the country. In the city formerly known as Constantinople they exist alongside the more specific habits of the *Istanbullu,* the people who identify as being of Istanbul, as well as with the regional traditions families bring with them when they migrate to the city and become part of the urban landscape. Particular methods of cooking or stories which tell of the past are kept within the family until they need to be brought out to celebrate a wedding or explain a connection. Migration, whether from within Turkey or from without, continues to play a significant part in shaping the cultural diversity of Istanbul. No matter how much the city tries, it remains a collection of villages, each with their own traditions and cultural markers, determined by the mix of individual populations rather than a quality inherent to the place.

When you ask a Turk living in Istanbul where they are from, they will most likely tell you the name of their *memleket,* their hometown. Few people I've ever met actually equate this with Istanbul, even if they live down the road from the hospital where they were born. No matter they have never been there, this connection with place of birth, their own or their parents, is very strong. This imbues the city with a sense of being an elsewhere, a place occupied by people aching with loss and longing for a mythical past that is somehow always better than the present. This intangible quality gives Istanbul a unique allure reminiscent of a lover long since gone. Along with the other inhabitants of Istanbul, I continue to follow the scents carried on the breeze hoping to find the source of the perfume.

Lemon Cologne

When I first lived in Turkey rather than staying here for a short time as a tourist, I spent hours in the cars of friends, driving from one side of the city to the other in search of the best. The best kebab, the best fish sandwiches, the best sweets and the best tea. It didn't matter if we were going to eat breakfast, lunch or dinner, there was always a particular place we absolutely had to go. At the time it seemed like an extraordinary amount of effort just to have something to eat, but over the years I've come to appreciate this attention to perfection. Once you've eaten the best *iskender kebab*, a Bursa specialty made up of wafer thin slices of *döner* meat on top of cubes of *pide* bread, topped with fresh tomato puree and yoghurt before being anointed with hot melted butter, sampled the best *lokum,* which for me has to be Turkish delight from Hacı Bekir, and drowned in the syrupy honey of the best *baklava*, from Gaziantep of course, your tastebuds will never be the same again. You'll rarely if ever let inferior quality products pass your lips and visiting friends will be lectured on the many reasons why you have to trek two hours across the city to eat at a specific establishment, as nothing else will do.

It's the same with drinking tea. There are many Turkish proverbs concerning tea, but my favourite comes from Sivas. There people say "*Çaysız sohbet, aysiz gök yüzü gibidir*", meaning "Conversations without tea are like a night sky without the moon". Although I'm a dedicated coffee drinker, when I'm with my best girlfriend Sonay I drink gallons of Turkish *çay*. We sit and talk and gossip and chatter for hours while sipping this jewel-like amber fluid served in small dainty glasses. Sonay says if I'd only learn to make Turkish tea myself I'd be a full-blown Turk. Although I do still forget the order of the tea making ritual, I know how I like to drink it. I always have it "*açık*", literally meaning 'light' in colour as the Turks express it, or 'weak' as we think about it in English. I also know a business meeting, no matter how tense, can't start unless you say yes to a glass of tea and at least take a sip. Up until that point conversation is strictly limited to the weather and if in Istanbul, the abominable state of the traffic that day, or any day in actual fact.

Turks and tea go together, and nowhere is this better illustrated than on the ferries that ply the Bosphorus, Golden Horn and Sea of Marmara. On even the shortest journey by ferry in Istanbul, the five minute crossing from Üsküdar to Beşiktaş, most Turks can manage to drink at least one glass of tea. When I regularly used to make the twenty minute journey from Kadıköy to Eminönü, I would marvel at how in that short time people could drink not one but two cups of tea, served in traditional delicate little tulip-shaped glasses, even when the boat was swaying heavily from side to side. The beverages were often accompanied by a freshly baked *simit*. These sourdough rings of heaven are so popular I suspect should supply be cut off one day, anarchy would break out. Back then people could still smoke on the ferries and had one if not two cigarettes per glass of tea as well. Sadly these days, the beautiful glasses which radiate the rich ruby colours of the tea are being replaced by more utilitarian paper cups. The tea might still be brewed the same way but the waxy coating of the cup changes the smell and the taste of this ubiquitous beverage.

Nonetheless, I doubt the Turkish passion for fruit will ever change. When *dut* season starts in Istanbul, I often only know from the rejected mulberries squashed into the pavement. Or from when I walk along, happily daydreaming, and am startled out of my reverie by the sudden rustling of the leaves on a tree in a garden I'm passing. One time this happened I looked up and saw a man just climbing down from a huge mulberry tree. He was dressed in a smart business suit complete with highly polished pointy shoes, munching away on the mulberries he had filched. On other occasions I've watched with amusement and concern as groups of men inadvisably prop rickety ladders against the flimsy upper branches of the fruit trees dotting the street. Along with the rapidly growing audience that always appears out of nowhere, I hold my breath and wait until one of them successfully or otherwise climbs to the top. All the while he will be directed as to his next move by his friends and anyone else who happens to be passing and feels qualified to comment.

Another example of this penchant for light fingered gardening is the housewifely tradition of making *yaprak sarma* or *yaprak dolma,* also known as dolmades, from grape leaves growing in the neighbours' yard. It's an accepted practice and the vine doesn't even have to cross the neighbours' fence to be fair game. I've seen women alight from cars and enter the gardens of apartment blocks, armed with empty plastic bags, ready to pick off the vine leaves. When caught red-handed they smile unashamedly and generously offer to share the harvest. I have to admit that the best *yaprak dolma* I've ever tasted were made by the mother of a friend of mine, who always picked the leaves from the neighbour's vine in the dead of night.

However, of all the traditions that say Turkey to me, the use of lemon cologne is the earliest and strongest memory I will always have. When I first came to the country back in 1990, I took long road trips on buses stinking of cigarette smoke. Despite the nicotine fug I always came out smelling of citrus. This was because after every stop we made, the bus boy walked along the aisle, proffering a bottle of strongly scented lemon cologne. By watching the other passengers I learnt to hold out my cupped hands into which he would sprinkle or indeed sometimes pour the liquid, depending on his enthusiasm and attention span.

A bottle of lemon cologne continues to be a much welcomed present from Turks visiting family living abroad, and mothers' often pack one in the luggage of a child setting off to study in another city. When sprinkled on the wrists the aroma works as a poignant yet comforting reminder of home. Sadly, like tea being served in real glass on the ferries, as Turkey embraces newer and more hygienic practices, in many cafes and restaurants bottles of lemon cologne are being replaced by small squares of freshness in the form of moist towelettes. Offered at the end of a meal, they still carry the same scent as before, but the solemn ritual of offering and receiving perfumed water from the bottle is lost.

In any other city when progress replaces history, the strength of symbols of the past can become fragile and eventually disappear over time. Not in Istanbul however, where a constant longing for the past is part and parcel of being an *Istanbullu*, a city dweller renowned for suffering from the melancholy of *hüzün*. As long as the roads of Istanbul are clogged with cars full of friends and relatives crisscrossing the city on the hunt for the best tasting pudding or the most delicious ice cream, these fragments of memory will always mean Turkey to me.

Best Foot Forward - Turkish Slippers

According to one Turkish proverb, cleanliness is a sign of faith. While the majority of Turks are Muslim and follow at least some of the tenants of Islam, the condition of public spaces around the country doesn't always seem to match this level of belief. There's often garbage on the streets in Istanbul and other Turkish towns and cities and people don't hesitate to casually drop rubbish on the ground. Coming from Australia, where anti-littering campaigns have been the norm for decades, and children are taught to care for the environment almost from the time they are born, it can be distressing. However I know public service announcements urging citizens to care for the environment have only started to appear on Turkish television in the last few years.

I also know that this behaviour isn't arbitrary. It relates to the way Turks view the world as being divided into outside, pubic space, and inside, private space. Public space is owned by everyone and therefore is the responsibility of no one. The state of private space, such as the inside of a person's home, must be and usually is immaculate. After the obligatory cleaning, one way of guaranteeing purity is to insist that anyone who steps foot inside your home wears slippers.

Wherever I've lived in Turkey, particularly in small towns, I've done a lot of visiting. Whether to see colleagues who'd married recently, someone recovering from an operation, or friends who'd just had a baby, a visit to someone was certain to occur every other week. My schooling in the etiquette of visiting began in Kayseri, a sprawling provincial capital on the rolling plains of central Anatolia. When I lived there, Kayseri was hot and dusty and the roads were under construction all year round. Although they were well graded from being redone the year before, the work was put out to tender annually and those seeking favours from the local authorities entered suspiciously low bids. Any items cemented into place, such as traffic lights, road signs and parking meters, were uprooted and sometimes placed tidily by the side of the street, but more usually were just haphazardly thrown onto the road. I could never understood why they installed parking meters in the first place. The minute anyone parked their car, a man wearing an official looking reflective vest with a bulky leather pouch strapped around his waist would appear. He'd give a ticket to the driver, and sometimes also took the car keys, to allow for double and even triple parking. On the driver's return whatever cash handed over was added to a wad of notes secreted away securely at the bottom of the parking man's bag.

It was never clear to me exactly why there were so many roadworks in Kayseri, but whatever the reason there was always something going on necessitating construction. As the roads were forever being torn up, smoothed and levelled bus routes were often redirected. While I enjoyed theses impromptu tours of previously unseen neighbourhoods in the town, I was less happy when the sidewalks were effected. Even when they weren't being fixed the pavements were hard to traverse. They were only easily accessible by those with long or strong legs because they were placed so high off the ground it was more a leap than a step up from the kerb. Pedestrians came low in the transport pecking order and I became adept at climbing over and around eruptions of brick work and at avoiding deep holes that appeared overnight without warning or sharp pieces of metal sticking out of the ground for no discernible reason. All this work involved a lot of noise and inconvenience and mud, which tangled with the dusty winds that regularly blew down from the three extinct volcanoes forming a triangle around the town. Unlike my more image conscious colleagues at the university where I worked, I couldn't be bothered to carry a shoe cleaning kit in my handbag so my shoes were perpetually dirty.

Anyone who's ever visited a Turkish home knows not to enter wearing outdoor shoes. Given the state of the pavements both in Kayseri and elsewhere in the country, and the fact that interior cleanliness is highly regarded in Turkey, this makes good sense. Shoes are automatically removed and left outside the door or inside the entry hall. Where they're placed depends as much on the security of the location as on the owner's obsession with order. After living in Turkey for a while you quickly learn to think about what shoes you plan to wear when you're going visiting, and the state of your socks or stockings. You don't want to be the last one standing alone on the door mat while the host hovers nearby, watching anxiously as you struggle to undo your complicated laces while everyone else is already seated inside. Even worse, once your shoes have finally joined the others in neat rows set out along the walls is not the time to discover the hole in your sock revealing a big toe, and if you're a woman, a big toenail unadorned by nail polish.

I don't like wearing slippers because my feet get hot easily, especially inside the overheated apartments favoured by Turks. However, unless the home owner is a good friend, it's nearly impossible to refuse the proffered slippers. Unfortunately too, form often follows function rather than style. I once spent an otherwise enjoyable night at the home of a student quietly ignoring the feelings of dismay that arose every time I caught sight of the chunky white, strappy, high-heeled sandals I had been given to wear with my all black outfit.

In recounting this fashion *faux pas* to my colleagues in Kayseri, I learnt that slippers can also be a fashion statement, and are sometimes more expensive than ordinary shoes. There are shops around the country devoted wholly to slippers, offering anything from flat practical models designed to warm the feet to luxurious pairs sporting spike heels, glitter and feathers. Married women from upper class families across the country spend a lot of their days and many of their evenings visiting. They have slippers to complement every outfit, carefully transported from home to home in a drawstring bag specially made to match their outfit. The very wealthy will even buy internationally famous brand name shoes and keep them solely for indoor use.

For families who employ a helper in their home, usually a woman who comes to clean, cook and possibly baby sit, it's normal for the employer to buy them slippers to wear on the job. The reasons will vary from situation to situation. It could be because they want her to feel welcome, they might worry she won't want to carry her own slippers with her every day from home or maybe they know she can't afford to buy herself a nice pair, befitting a guest in their home.

At the other end of the spectrum is the toilet slipper. In many homes the toilet is housed in a separate room to the bathroom. Rather than a sit down toilet known to the Turks as *ala Franga* style, literally meaning French toilet, you're faced with a toilet pan at floor level, designed to be employed using the squat method. The cistern is frequently housed very high up the wall with either no chain or one so short as to be unreachable. Therefore flushing is achieved by filling a plastic jug from a low tap installed for just this purpose and washing the bowl clean. Unfortunately, no matter how hard the occupants try, the floor surrounding the toilet pan will be left awash with clean water, hence the presence of plastic scuffs just inside the door. Aside from the fact that they've been bought to fit the largest feet in the house, they're often wet. Clean but soggy. It requires some skill to put them on without getting your socks or stockings wet and to then negotiate the task of completing the act you came in for, all without letting anything touching the ground.

What I learned in Kayseri has stood me in good stead for life in Istanbul. While I tend to go out with my friends to cafes, restaurants and bars, I still spend time at their homes with their mums and grandmothers. Naturally they always insist I wear slippers inside, as I now do when people come to visit me. It's generally believed one will get ill if slippers are not worn, and I've long since given up trying to convince my friends otherwise. To be polite guests first ask if they should leave their shoes outside the apartment door to ensure absolutely no dirt comes inside. They know the apartment will be spotless because naturally the host will have spent the day before cleaning everything in sight. I hate housework but love entertaining guests, so I clean thoroughly because it feels like I'm being rewarded for my labours rather than just moving the dirt around. I even clean the bathroom, even though in the two whole years I lived in Kayseri, not one of my guests ever used it. Even in Istanbul, only after repeated visits and earnest reassurances do my closest of friends do more in there than wash their hands.

I always bring their shoes inside my apartment because if I don't the building caretaker knocks on my door to lecture me. According to him thieves will come in to steal all the footwear although I'm not sure how they'll get in through the locked downstairs security door. I bought special mats to put down for events when I'm expecting a lot of people. That way I can line up everyone's shoes along the hallway without discomforting them by putting their soiled footwear directly onto my clean floors.

Now I too have slippers at the ready for my guests. I have winter slippers and summer slippers, fancy leather slippers from Morocco and slippers worn by shepherds from Kahramanmaraş that have never touched grass or even seen a sheep. My hall cupboard holds two shoe horns, a short one to use when you're sitting down to put your shoes on and a long one for those who prefer to put their shoes on standing up, or are too old or incapacitated to easily reach their feet. Every few years I buy new family packs of slippers offering mum, dad, big brother, big sister and little sibling sized slippers, so I'm ready for any eventuality. Whether it's too hot, they're too small, or clash dreadfully with your outfit, slippers are *de rigueur* when you visit a Turkish home.

Your Future in a Coffee Cup - Fal

One enduring memory people take away with them after their first visit to Turkey is of breakfast. They speak in almost awed tones of hotel buffets overflowing with food, and assume all Turks sit down to a similar array every day. Sadly, the reality is that during the week most Istanbul residents rise early, wash and quickly dress before running out the door to catch a service bus to work. These buses traverse a fixed path, picking up other employees from the same company, and can take up to two hours to complete their route. Consequently most of my Turkish friends say it's so early when they have to get up they can't face food. It's not until they get to the office that they grab a bite to eat. *Poğaça*, a type of small savoury pastry, are very popular in the morning and they'll eat a couple at their desk before starting work. Weekends are another matter though and breakfast, or rather brunch, is almost an institution. Indeed so popular is brunch that many restaurants offer special weekend all-you-can-eat-deals, and a well-known website regularly features brunch discount coupons. These are mainly available in spring and autumn because a lot of Istanbul residents go to their holiday houses during the summer months, while the cold of winter keeps them at home. Most brunches happen on Sundays, when everyone sleeps in and gets up ready to dedicate the day to catching up with family and friends. The best brunches end with *fal,* the age old art of having your future read from the patterns formed by the coffee grinds left in your coffee cup. However this being Turkey, where food is second in importance only to family, first you have to give the food the attention it deserves.

A typical brunch spread will include ripe red tomatoes tasty enough to eat without salt, fresh crunchy peeled cucumbers, black and green olives steeped in oil and fresh herbs, cheese of all descriptions such as the ordinary white Turkish cheese similar to fetta, salty *tulum* made from goat's milk and cured in the same animal's skin, or the aesthetically pleasing but mild tasting plaited white cheese called *Diyabakır örgü.* These standards will always be accompanied by more substantial fare. At the very least there will be a choice of boiled eggs, omelettes, *menemen,* a spicy egg and tomato favourite of mine, or *sucuklu yumurta,* fatty spicy sausages highly prized in central Turkey fried in with eggs. The last two items are both cooked in tin lined copper dishes called *sahan* and brought straight to the table, blisteringly hot and mouth-wateringly good. Those with a sweet tooth can indulge in honey on the comb or jams made from rose petals and any of the stone fruits, served with a healthy dollop of *kaymak,* the Turkish version of clotted cream. All this is eaten with copious slices of fresh bread. In the past there was only crusty white bread available, baked twice daily, but these days you can choose from white, wholemeal, rye, bran or *simit,* traditional Turkish sourdough rings sprinkled with sesame seeds. Naturally the whole lot is washed down by as many glasses of Turkish tea as you can manage. Most brunch deals include *sınırsız* tea, a limitless supply, which comes in handy for my friends who can drink more than ten glasses in one sitting.

These lazy Sunday mornings stretch into endless afternoons where you eat too much, gossip a lot, and just enjoy yourself. Then, after everyone has eaten enough and drunk their last glass of tea, it's time for coffee. Coffee is drunk according to personal taste, so while I like mine *orta şekerli,* with medium sugar, others like theirs *sade,* black or even very sweet, called *şekerli.* Deciding how you like your coffee is the easy part, because *fal* isn't as simple as swirling the leftover coffee grounds around and describing what you see. There's a strict procedure that must be followed if your future is to be revealed.

When the coffee is finished, you have to place the saucer upside down on top of the cup, and make a wish. Then, carefully hold the cup in the air with one or both hands and solemnly turn it anti-clockwise three times. Next turn the cup and saucer back over, so the cup is upside down on the saucer, and leave it to cool. Some women like to tap the bottom of the cup while others place their wedding ring on the cup, because they believe doing so cools the coffee down faster. It's also believed that placing a ring on the cup ensures revelations about your love life. Similarly, placing a coin on the cup not only cools it faster but is thought to dispel bad omens. When the coffee cup is cool enough, someone other than the person who drank the coffee starts reading the shapes made by the left over the coffee grounds.

For fortune telling, the coffee cup is read in two horizontal halves because it speaks of both the past and the future. The shapes in the lower half talk of the past, while those in the top half speak of the future. The shapes that feature on the right side are usually understood positively, while the shapes on the left side are understood as signs of bad events, enemies, illnesses, troubles, and so on. According to another belief, the coffee cup can tell the past but it can only tell forty days into the future. There are a whole series of shapes and signs with particular meanings but in general they speak of travel, money, gifts, friendship, love, weddings and marriage.

One's future isn't just written inside the cup. If the cup and the saucer are firmly stuck together, and the *falcı*, the person reading your *fal,* is having trouble separating them, it is believed that this particular cup should not be read. This is known as a case of "prophet's fortune telling". The person who has drunk from the cup is considered lucky, and therefore does not need to have their fortune read. Similarly if a large amount of coffee grounds fall into the saucer when the cup is being separated, the interpretation is that the owner of the cup will soon have no more troubles or sadness. According to another standard interpretation, if coffee drips onto the saucer as the cup is opened, the person who drank it will soon cry.

After the interpretation of the shapes within the cup, it's time to interpret the shapes in the saucer, where the majority of the coffee grounds will be found. The saucer is generally understood as the home of the person whose cup is being read. If there are large areas on the saucer with no coffee on them, the interpretation is that life in the person's home will be easy. If the shapes on the saucer are confused and messy, this is taken to mean that there will be a funeral or illness-related crowd in this person's house. During this part of the reading, the person telling the fortune holds the saucer up so it is vertical, and waits for coffee grounds and coffee to flow. At the end of the reading, the saucer is turned over once. At this stage, if a drop of coffee manages to get behind, and half way into the saucer's radius, this is taken as a sign that the wish made will come true.

My coffee cup, when opened for a reading, usually contains large blocky shapes which to my eye reveal nothing. However there is always someone at our brunch table who has a natural talent for *fal,* and many times I've listened intently to promises of better times, new friendships and more travel. I can't say I'm one hundred percent convinced that what I learn through *fal* is reliable but I know I can always have another cup of coffee if I don't like what I hear. Besides, *fal* is as much about spending time with my friends as it is with telling my fortune, because their company and loyalty speak volumes about what my future holds.

A Touch of Spice

In a little known film set in Istanbul spanning the last century, herbs and spices play an important role. They represent the continuity of history as well as the diversity within cultures. After interviewing my *baharatçı,* my spice seller Ayhan Baloğlu, I can see why. Born in Gaziantep on the hot dusty plains of south eastern Turkey, young Ayhan came to Istanbul in 1985. He started his apprenticeship in the wholesale district of Eminönü in 1990, learning the craft directly from his master in the traditional way. Over time he went from uncertainly following orders to fill bags with herbs and spices while listening intently to the information that came with them, to himself instructing his apprentice on which balms to recommend for what ailment. From day one Ayhan supplemented his knowledge by studying independently. He opened his own retail shop on the Asian side of Istanbul in Kadıköy in 2002. Called *Baloğlu*, literally meaning 'son of honey', it is tucked away on bustling Güneşlibahçe Sokak, better known as Fish Street. From his brightly lit and well laid out store Ayhan dispenses herbs and advice in equal measure.

We began our interview sitting on low stools at the back of the shop. Slowly stirring sugar into my tea I asked him to name the ten bestselling herbs and spices. Without hesitation he listed "black pepper, ginger, cinnamon, turmeric, pine nuts for stuffed vegetables, dried red pepper flakes, white pepper, flax seeds, black cumin and thyme". He explained that most Turks wouldn't have all these things in their kitchen at the same time but said, "Without a doubt you'll find black pepper, dried red pepper flakes, the herbs and spices used for making plain tomato paste or the hot and spicy variety, as well as cinnamon, ginger, turmeric and black cumin seeds".

At first glance Turkish kitchens appear to offer far fewer choices of cuisine than mine. I'm from Australia and our diet is influenced by a multicultural population. It's not unusual to have Thai one night and Middle Eastern the next. I have to confess though, this isn't because I'm such an enthusiastic cook. My husband is the one always trying out new recipes and taste sensations. My job is to go out and gather the ingredients. Kim loves to make curry from scratch and I remember being frustrated when I couldn't locate any turmeric in our early days in Turkey. All I could find were packets of ready-made curry powder in the supermarket that lacked the bite we prefer. Of course, over time I learnt I should be looking for the ingredients in a *baharatçı*, the Turkish word meaning both the name of the place selling herbs and spices, as well as the person selling them. Even though I knew I could find a wide variety of spices in his shop, I was really surprised to hear Ayhan mention turmeric, because none of my Turkish friends use it. When he told me it was mainly found in a few desserts and even then only to provide colour, I understood why I'd thought the Turkish kitchen limited.

It's not just foreigners who suffer from a lack of awareness about the cornucopia of herbs and spices available in Turkey. When I mentioned tarragon, called *tarhun* in Turkish, to seven of my female Turkish friends, I had to repeat the word several times before they were satisfied I had the pronunciation right. Finally, all but one admitted they'd never heard of it. The one who had was the daughter of a musician in the army. Her childhood was spent moving to a new place in Turkey every few years, so she has had more exposure to all the foodstuffs Turkey has to offer than the average Turk.

When I told Ayhan this story he laughed, and replied, "Of course they don't know about it. Tarragon comes from the south east of Turkey. It's a characteristic of the Gaziantep kitchen and is only used there. It isn't a herb that's known about in a lot of regions in Turkey. In Gaziantep it's used in soup or in a particular type of *köfte*, actually it's used in a lot of meatballs. However only those who know about tarragon use it. Outside of that it's only known to a few people through word of mouth or from the people who come to Gaziantep and transport it to other places." He went on to explain that the range of herbs in Turkey is considerable, but their use and availability are often limited to the regions from where they originate. One example is the group of herbs and greens belonging to the Mediterranean and the Aegean provinces. There green basil, sweet purple basil, wild greens, onions, garlic and other vegetables from the same family are used in particular ways that are quite specific to those areas. After listening to Ayhan I realised once again the importance of never assuming things in Turkey are the same as back home. I've known for a long time that Bursa is famous for its peaches and Çanakkale for its apples, and now I recognize that the geography of Turkey can also be traced through its herbs and spices.

I asked Ayhan whether he would describe himself as a shop owner or as an *aktar*, an alternative word to *baharatçı*, meaning healer. He unhesitatingly responded with *aktar* and declared, "Herbs are extremely useful I believe, because the pharmacological source of medicines is herbs. There are herbs in them". He added "If we want to know what herbs we can use from the environment, which ones are the most beneficial, we should know which products we should use and how to use them so we won't be ill. I think people wouldn't even go to the doctor if they knew about herbal medicines but I don't think many people think the same way. In my opinion the first cause of illness is stress and the second is a diet high in sugar. People with high blood sugar don't look very well and their health is now being destroyed by fast food. It is very damaging ... Their health deteriorates very slowly over time as they age. I am very rarely ill, I always look after myself and do what is beneficial for my health and well-being."

It is clear Ayhan feels strongly about the benefits of herbal medicines, but admits general knowledge about the wealth of herbs available in Turkey is still quite narrow. He is optimistic this is changing as communication about the existence and usefulness of regional herbs is beginning to spread. "People are starting to use herbal remedies more and to ask what is this, what is that, and other similar questions. In the last few decades for example, fresh ginger has been introduced to Turkey. Perhaps in Europe and America people have used ginger for many years but here it is more recent. In addition, people are becoming inspired to go to specialists or overseas for new health remedies."

He added a word of warning however, about the rising popularity of different forms of alternative medicines. He is concerned that when people hear about them from others, the information they receive could be wrong. In particular, he mentioned dosage and advised people to do a test before taking a remedy, to see how they will react. "I believe," he told me, "people need to read up on the subject and to educate themselves more. Treatments should be based on good education and thorough research." These are wise words indeed from someone who has always practised what he preaches.

When Writing Crosses Borders

When I started writing my blog about Turkey, it was with the idea of sharing my thoughts and experiences. I hoped to give people an idea of what everyday life is like for an expat in Istanbul. Many of my posts have made people laugh, and a few have made them think, leading them to buy my books in search of answers to questions they didn't know they had. After reading my essays, some of them want to meet me because my words strike a cord with something in their lives. Often women, these readers are at a crossroads, and want to know whether to play it safe or dive into the deep end. As a person who doesn't see packing up all their worldly goods and moving to the other side of the world as a risk, I'm probably not the best person to ask. Notwithstanding, living in such a foreign culture has made me reflect on my own life, and really question who I am. I now know what values I hold dear and those on which I won't compromise. Maybe, for people who don't really know where they are in their own lives, that's why meeting someone like me appeals.

I recently met up with one such reader in Sultanahmet, the Istanbul neighbourhood which is home to the old city, and popular with the majority of tourists. I had 'talked' with 'Grubana"* a few times on Facebook, and we'd agreed to meet outside the Istanbul Sultanahmet Vakfı, a charitable religious foundation. Before going I checked out the *vakfı* website and discovered it was located in the Little Haghia Sophia neighbourhood, a few streets behind the Hippodrome. Arriving at the address I'd written down I discovered the foundation is actually in the Şehit Mehmed Sokullu Paşa Camii complex. Comprising a mosque and *medrese*, a theological school where Koran courses are now taught, this establishment was designed by the famous Turkish architect Mimar Sinan at the request of Sultana Esma. She was the daughter of Sultan Selin II and ordered the mosque be built for her husband Sokullu Mehmed, a Grand Vizier of Serbian origin.

I saw there were two entryways for the mosque, a small one on the street I'd walked down, and another grander entry gate around the corner and down a hill. I chose to stand outside the lower entrance. As I waited I noted the shabbiness of the street and the insalubrious nature of the air. Across from where I was standing, two unshaven men were hanging around outside a barber shop. I covertly watched them as they tried not to let on they were watching

*name changed to protect her privacy.

me. Further down the hill the cries of neighbourhood kids playing football reassured me I wasn't completely alone, but as the minutes ticked by I had to wonder if my reader was going to turn up. As I pondered the surprisingly village feel of the area, with its small row of local shops selling bread, meat and vegetables, I noticed the road across from me was called Özbekler Sokak, which means Uzbek Street in English. Given that street names in Istanbul almost always reflect the origins of the inhabitants or their trade, I have to assume it used to be home to an Uzbek population. Even though the damp was beginning to seep up painfully from the old worn stones and into my feet, I was pleased by my discovery and wondered what else I'd learn today.

After fifteen minutes the cold called for action so I walked back up the slope and went into a design school housed in an Ottoman building opposite the mosque, to ask if anyone there knew about another branch of the foundation. *"Maalesef"*, they said, unfortunately they didn't, so I wandered into the small rain washed marble courtyard of the mosque to see what I could learn there. According to an inscription dating to 1571, the mosque was built on the site of a former church but there is no sign of that now. All I saw were five or six tourists, armed with long lens cameras, waiting in the bleak winter sun for prayers to end. Once inside they would marvel at the majestic architectural lines of Sinan's design, and look for pieces of the *Kaaba* interred in the *minber*, the ornate pulpit mainly used for Friday prayers.

Along the wall facing the entry to the mosque I noticed the condensation covered windows of the *medrese*. Peering through them I saw cushions on the ground in front of a number of *rahle*, low bookrests used for holding the Koran, and spied a computer monitor in the distance. The young man working at it responded to my insistent tapping on the glass, quickly jumping up and coming over to see what I wanted. I soon learned that although their website listed no other location, at least as far as I could understand, there was also another branch at its namesake the Sultanahmet Camii.

If you haven't been to Sultanahmet Camii, also known as the Blue Mosque, it's huge, and sits in an even larger courtyard. As soon as I reached the external wall I asked about the whereabouts of the *vakfı* again. Even though I had already been told there was another branch here, this being Turkey, I needed to checked the information at least three times to be sure. The *simit* seller I spoke to said there was no *vakfı* here, but there was a *dernek,* otherwise known as an association. Did I mean this, he questioned. Turks aren't great lateral thinkers but I am, so I said yes, hoping I was right.

I followed his directions but almost immediately became lost amongst the hundreds of tourists, in groups, pairs or alone, milling around, taking group shots, selfies and artistic images, obscuring any chance I had of finding a sign to show where my reader was waiting. At another entry in the exterior wall, I asked a third man, a security guard this time, for more directions. He too thought there was a *dernek* but not a *vakfı* somewhere in the grounds and took off in search of it. As he scurried away to the other end of the gardens I began to despair of ever finding Grubana. All the same I followed in his wake, determined not to give up. Suddenly he came to an abrupt halt and told me he was going to check with a colleague before darting into a low building tucked away in a stand of trees. Within a few minutes he returned and told me yes, there was a *vakfı*. Apologetically he said he hadn't known about it because he was new. I thanked him for his help before hurrying off in the direction he indicated and almost immediately found Grubana, my reader, standing in front of a startling white building with letters four feet high saying 'Istanbul Sultanahmet Vakfı'. It seemed a little odd that people who'd been working in the complex for years weren't aware of such an imposing structure but then again I knew of the Turkish tendency to fixate on exact meanings of words and to only inquire about something if they had an immediate need of the knowledge. Thankfully I had the excuse that I'd missed it because I'd walked through the Hippodrome and not past the front of the Blue Mosque.

Over coffee I told Grubana of the mix-up over the location of the foundation. When I told her I had discovered the mosque I'd first been waiting at was built for a Turkish Grand Vizier of Serbian descent she surprised me by telling me she already knew. It turned out Grubana is from Belgrade where the story of Mehmed Sokullu is well known through a novel written by the Serbian author Ivo Andric. Called *The Bridge on the Drina*, the book is set in the city of Vizegrad and tells the tale of a small Serbian boy taken from his mother to be given to the Sultan. This practice, called *devşirme,* roughly translates as 'tribute in blood', whereby the Ottoman Empire sent soldiers to abduct boys, who were the sons of their Christian subjects, from the villages of the Balkans and other territories. They were then converted to Islam and the ablest children trained for the army or the civil service. The majority of them became members of the Janissary corps, an elite group that formed the troops and bodyguards of the Ottoman Sultans.

The boy's mother, like all the mothers of these children, follows her son, weeping at the thought of losing him. They reach the river where the children are taken by ferry to the other side, leaving the grieving mothers behind. After becoming Muslims the boys take a Turkish name. Mehmed as he is now known, rises quickly up the ranks and around the age of sixty becomes the Grand Vizier. Holding this position for almost fifteen years, he played a crucial role in the expansion campaigns of three Ottoman sultans. Yet his separation from his mother still haunted him and he decided to order the building of a bridge at the point on the river where they were parted. Construction of the actual bridge began in 1571 and was completed in 1577. Ivo Anric's novel won the Nobel Peace Prize for Literature in 1961, and it stands as a lasting testament to Serbian history and his literary skills. Similarly, the bridge over the River Drina, called the Mehmed Paša Sokolović Bridge, stands as a memorial to the country's long and turbulent history.

Now, rather than remembering this as a meeting where I had to stand out in the cold due to a misunderstanding, I see it as a series of startling but pointed coincidences. First I went to Turkish Sultanahmet to meet a foreigner, and found myself in an area that was once home to Uzbeks, foreigners themselves, at a mosque built for a Serb. I then learnt the story of this mosque, built for Mehmed Sokullu, from a person of Serbian descent. These things happened for a reason, but it is up to us to work out why. Just as my writing helps me move from the past and set the course for a happier and more satisfying future, I think it also acts as a bridge for Grubana and others like her to overcome their fear of change to seek out new possibilities and ways of being.

Freestyle or Overarm - the Language of Swimming

Being Australian and living in Istanbul, at first one of the hardest things to cope with was the difficulty of finding a pool to go swimming in regularly. Prior to 1980 life in Istanbul had been much like life in Sydney. People spent their summer days swimming at beaches along the Sea of Marmara and their evenings at outdoor cinemas. Locally produced wine was plentiful and mixed sex events the norm. Cue the military coup and over the ensuing years Turkey regressed in many ways. By the time I came to live here again in 2010, things had eased up a lot, but finding somewhere to swim was still problematic.

I'm used to pay-as-you-go pools, but here you don't have that choice. You can join in with monthly classes, segregated by sex, at set times, or pay for quarterly, half or full year memberships where you can swim in mixed pools but again, only at fixed times. I already know how to swim and my plans frequently change so neither option suited me. After much research I found a pool which offered entry whenever I chose at a reasonable price.

Initially I was just so excited to find somewhere to train that I paid little attention to my fellow swimmers. I would go to the pool between appointments, complete one kilometre as quickly as my body allowed, then hop in the shower, get dressed and take off for my next meeting. Over time however, I began to notice startling differences in both the techniques and the outfits of the other people in the pool with me. I came to realise you could tell when people had first begun swimming by their bathing attire and sometimes even fairly accurately surmise their personal history and beliefs.

There are old men who are happy to show their limbs, wearing short-legged trunks that sit high up over their navels. Strange as it might sound, this willingness to expose their legs is a sign they grew up holding the values of Atatürk, the founder of the modern Turkish republic, close to their hearts. They are the portlier Turkish versions of young Italian boys from daring movies of the 1950s. Each time I touch the wall before turning to start the next lap I see them lined up at the edge of the pool, solemnly bending at the knees, before stretching out their arms at the completion of each squat. Only after they've finished at least twenty minutes of stretches accompanied by strenuous breathing do they enter the pool. Once they've taken careful measure of the space available to them and considered the temperature they plod along using a stroke that looks like a distant relation to dog paddle.

In other lanes vast old ladies, so broad in the beam that one on her own takes up the whole width, bathe rather than swim. They wear voluminous one-piece costumes dating from the 1960s, sporting modesty skirts, the flounces of which match their fashionable bathing caps dotted with gaudy flowers. When I race along in the next lane I see their dismay when my confident strokes displace too much water and threaten to splash their carefully made up faces. Their *Istanbullu* accents and the careful way they articulate each word tell me they come from old Ottoman families. That and the drivers waiting out front in shiny black cars ready to take them to the hairdresser for a blow-dry after each swim.

No one sports the string bikinis I remember my older sister wearing in the 1970s. This is possibly because they unravelled from use or maybe due to the civil unrest of the decade which meant swimming was the last thing on people's minds. Nor does anyone wear ostentatious cutaway diamante disasters popular in the 1980s. While this could be due to politics, I think it's more likely because those Dallas and Dynasty style costumes weren't actually designed for swimming in, only to be seen.

Back in 1990 when I went to the Princess Islands for the first time I saw a woman wearing such an outfit, lounging by the water's edge, the sun painfully reflecting off the sparkly detailing. Given the rigidity of her blow dried hair, I doubt she ever got wet. She was much like the women who come to my pool and sit about in towels and dressing gowns before lowering themselves carefully into the pool. First of course they have to complain at length about the temperature which I often find so high that I sweat as I do my laps. Once fully immersed up to their necks they cling to the edge, gossiping and getting in my way.

Then there are the men who unselfconsciously show off the thick swirls of hair adorning their belly buttons but make sure their knees are out of sight in long flappy versions of board shorts. They wear rubber caps to control their generous forests of head hair but their thick beards are left free to gently bob up and down in the water. From the way they clumsily breaststroke on the spot I can safely hazard a guess they only started swimming in the last few years, and not before they had consulted at length with both their imam and their doctor.

Lastly there are the women in their twenties wearing slickly daring racing back Speedos with silicone caps and goggles that transform them into squinty eyed fish. Few in number they mercilessly slap out their laps before transforming themselves into up and coming business women in the change rooms.

And as for me I hear you ask. Form follows function in the pool so I wear an unfashionably sturdy chlorine-resistant black one-piece, silicone cap, goggles and ear plugs. On summer holidays at the beach though it's another matter entirely.

Dancing in the Streets

One Saturday last summer I was on the phone chatting with my ninety four year old auntie in Australia. She and I love to talk and can do so for hours but this time I was distracted. The sound of drumming was coming from outside my window. At first the noise was muffled and indistinct but by the time I hung up it was almost deafening. I was confused. Ramazan had finished the previous month so it couldn't be that. Besides, the Ramazan drummers only came in the early hours of the morning to wake every one up for *sahur*, the meal before dawn. Now it was the middle of the day and I had no idea what was going on. I looked out the window and to my amazement saw two men spinning and whirling around in the middle of the street wearing long colourful skirts. They were accompanied by another two men beating time on large *davul,* traditional drums covered with goat skin. As the dancers wove in and out of a circle of onlookers the drummers swooped and bowed in time with the music.

Grabbing my camera I ran downstairs and joined Selim the waterman, Süleyman the tailor and Kamil our *kapıcı,* or doorman. They were watching the dancers in the company of the other *kapıcı* from our street, all of them smoking and chatting amongst themselves. When I eagerly asked about the skirt-wearing men, everyone was highly amused at how excited I was. Laughing kindly at my question Selim informed me they were from Sinop in the Black Sea region of Turkey and were here to help celebrate a wedding. Soon after the bride came out of the building two doors down from mine, a solid girl wrapped in metres of white satin, flanked by stout matrons in tight, shiny mother-of-the-bride cocktail dresses attended by young girls fluttering around them like butterflies dressed in brightly coloured concoctions of tulle and lace. Although now more generally associated with folk dancing and wedding celebrations, the tradition of male dancers, or *rakkas* as they are called in Turkish from the word *raks* meaning 'to dance', dates back to the seventeenth century.

Historians say there were two different kinds of *rakkas*, called *tavşan oğlan* and *köçek*. A *tavşan oğlan*, literally meaning 'rabbit boy', wore a stylish hat and tight pants, while *köcek* had long curly hair and wore women's clothes. Both performed at weddings in the past when strict gender segregation was applied to festivities, with men and women celebrating separately. They also performed at feasts, festivals and in the presence of the sultans. The majority of the rabbit boys are believed to have originated from non-Muslim societies living on islands in the Aegean and Marmara regions. Little else is known of them, in contrast to the well-documented history of the *köçek*. Originally sponsored by Ottoman sultans, pretty boys around the ages of seven or eight were chosen from non-Muslim populations across the vast Turkish Empire to be schooled in the art of dance. Muslims were forbidden to work as dancers during this era. The children trained for around six years before beginning to perform as fully fledged *köçek*. Their performances were described as being "sensuous, attractive and effeminate". They would enticingly gyrate their hips in the slow vertical and horizontal figure eight movements found in oriental or so called belly dance, snapping their fingers and making suggestive gestures. Although extremely skilled in dance the *köçek* were also available sexually, often going to the highest bidder and taking the passive role. Before long the art of the *köçek* moved from behind the protected walls of the Ottoman palaces out into *meyhane,* or drinking establishments, to reach a wider audience. Many of the most famous of these dancers were of Greek, Croat and Armenian descent and they became so popular they inadvertently incited male customers to fight for their favours. It became so bad that *köçek* performances were eventually outlawed in 1837.

The sexual nature of the art of oriental dance in Turkey and Middle Eastern countries is almost always the first aspect to be highlighted in Western representations of belly dancing. However the focus is on women performing the dance, not men. Popular images of Turkey feature scantily clad girls moving seductively to the pulsating rhythm of the *darbuka*, although in reality most girls dance privately in the company of women at weddings, rather than publicly for men. Belly dancing shows continue to be put on for tourists in Sultanahmet and Taksim, however more often than not these days they feature women from Russia and the Balkan states. Ironically, their blond hair and blue eyes greatly appeal to the ever-increasing number of Arab tourists visiting Turkey, much as they did when Circassian women were sold into the harems of the sultans.

In contrast, in the nightclubs frequented by my Turkish girlfriends, the trend is towards male dancers. One friend I take oriental dance classes with regularly frequents clubs offering male go-go dancers dressed only in skin-tight near indecent gold lame short shorts. As her grandmother doesn't even really approve of her granddaughter attending belly dancing classes I can't imagine what she'd say if she saw the provocative crotch shots I get on Facebook after a Saturday night out. Elsewhere, more upmarket venues are now entertaining their clientele by hosting male belly dancers. Either called *rakkas* or *zenne,* the latter translating literally as drag queen or female impersonator, the shows featuring men are now more popular than those performed by women.

When the art form was outlawed in the nineteenth century, the tradition of male dancers nearly died out, and only continued to take place in the privacy of people's homes in the north and south-eastern rural areas of the country. Then about fifteen years ago young men began to perform in public again. The internet was introduced to Turkey around this time, making non-Turkish films and music much more accessible, and the children of Turks who'd gone to live in Europe as guest workers in the 1960s and 1970s were coming of age and visiting their parents' hometowns, bringing with them new influences and different social mores.

Although the number of men performing oriental dance has risen, the stigma of doing so largely remains. Other than well-known names such as Mehmet Sasmaz, who dances under the stage name Zadiel. and performers such as Segah, most dancers hide how they make a living from their parents, particularly from their fathers. Yet *zenne* as they are now more commonly called without the derogative associations, have become the darlings of the well-to-do. They are invited to dance at private gatherings, for birthdays, weddings, circumcision ceremonies and at henna nights, the Turkish version of a hen's night or bridal shower. Surprisingly, even conservative families who would be unlikely to approve of go-go dancers and be horrified at the idea male strippers are comfortable with a *zenne* because even their grandmother is happy to dance along with them.

The heavily stubbled faces and Turkish balcony stomachs of the dancers in my street were vastly different to the slender young boys of past centuries with curly locks falling to their shoulders and the more recent versions sporting closely cropped hair and a well sculpted five o'clock shadow. The Sinop men, in their colourful multilayered skirts worn over black pants and white shirts were almost aggressively masculine with their solid dance steps and assertive manner, yet they shimmied their shoulders and clicked their castanets with a definite feminine grace. As I watched them twirl joyfully around the bride, the distinction between the past and the present slowly blurred, as it so often does in the suburbs of Istanbul..

Shopping for Unmentionables

As a young teenager I was a tomboy, so getting my first bra wasn't something I looked forward to. When the fateful day came my mum took me to a long established Sydney department store for a proper fitting. There we were looked after by a woman with an enormous shelf-like bust. On this rested a chain attached to eyeglasses propped onto the end of her nose, framed by a measuring tape draped around her neck. Instructing me to take off my T-shirt she quickly whipped the tape around me, all the while commenting to my mum about youth, size and perkiness, punctuated by intermittent laughter. Already feeling mortified, I remember just wanting to die when she helped me put on the bra by popping her hands into the cups to ensure I had it on properly, lifting and plumping up my adolescent breasts in the process.

Fast forward some twenty years later to Kayseri, central Turkey, where I discovered men and not women working in underwear shops. Despite the fact I wasn't brave enough to venture into any of the shops I saw, those intense feelings of embarrassment immediately came flooding right back. They increased even more when I learnt the men just had to scrutinize you closely to determine your size. If budget was an issue, you could always buy a bra at most weekly outdoor markets, where the procedure was very similar only with a much larger audience. Even today whole stalls are dedicated to underwear, with white cottontails forming neat rows next to see-through lace thongs drowning in bells and bows, framed by super hero boxer shorts on one side and Disney princess panties on the other. All the bras on offer are pegged onto a rope forming an arc overhead, organised according to the lingerie rainbow of red satin, yellow, green or blue polyester, white *broderie anglaise* bridal, black lace, leopard or tiger skin print bedroom. Two or three men stand behind the counter, eager to bag your selection, take your money, or correct you on your choice of size. No matter the professional face they present in these transactions, I still don't feel comfortable buying underwear from them.

Regardless of venue, the idea is that you buy the bra size the seller suggests and try it on at home. If they were wrong you can take the bra back and exchange it for one with a better fit. As a result there is no limit to the number of times people have told me to wash any new bra really well before wearing it, because there's no way of knowing how many people have already worn it. I've never asked if the same applies to underpants bought from the markets because I really don't want to know.

Now I live in Istanbul. While I can buy bras from my local outdoor market, I prefer to purchase them in modern, anonymous seeming department stores. I've overcome my initial tomboy resistance to the idea of wearing them and now choose luxurious underwear over utilitarian garments, but my early shyness about discussing underwear preferences remains. It's hard enough talking about what I like without doing it as a foreigner with an imperfect grasp of the language. To make matters worse I'm Australian and Turkish fashions are very different from ours, as are body shapes. I have broad shoulders and a strong torso, whereas Turkish women generally have narrow sloping shoulders atop thin petite frames. Finding a style I like, let alone one that fits me, is always a challenge.

Recently I went to my favourite shop and flicked through the bras on offer. The racks were full of limpid pastels and insipid shades of nude, ecru and washed out coffee, but I wanted something bright and bold. While I was hovering around the displays, trapped by my indecision, a sales assistant pounced. On hearing of my dilemma she said, yes, I did have broad shoulders and small breasts, so I could do with some more support and bolstering. Just in case I hadn't understood her Turkish, she firmly grasped the objects in question, one in each hand, and pushed them high up on my chest to demonstrate her point.

Biting down on the chagrin her comments and actions caused, I stayed true to my promise to try new things and break out of my comfort zone. For the next forty minutes I tried on an array of bras whether or not I liked the fabric, the colour or the style. After a while I was excited to hear her tap on the change room door so I could open it and see what new goodies she had to offer. When I finally left the shop I was happily clutching a bag containing a bra and knicker set in deep purple that offered the magic she promised to find me.

In contrast, buying underwear at an *Alış Veriş Merkezi*, the small local neighbourhood shops given the grand title of 'Shopping Centre', which sell everything from extension cords to dinner sets, is a different experience all together. Unmentionables, whether for men, women or children, really are unmentionable in this type of shop in Turkey. Underpants, singlets and bras are either safely hidden away on a mezzanine floor or out of sight down the back, so you have to already know where they are or send out a search party to find them. Glimpsing piles of socks and tights indicates you're going in the right direction, but some stores even have screens to shield the unsuspecting from accidentally catching sight of these forbidden items. When you've made your choice from a selection that usually ranges from virginal white, fire engine red or silky black trousseau wear, you have to wait for a girl to come and wrap them in opaque tissue paper. She places the price stickers on the outside and only then can you descend the stairs and head for the cash desk, where you hand over your packet, careful not to catch the eye of the man who is trying not to show he knows what you've bought.

Naturally I learnt about this system when I took some underpants straight downstairs, naked and exposed, and handed them directly to the man at the cash desk. He looked at me in horror and demanded to know why they weren't wrapped. While I stood at the cash desk trying to unravel his Turkish and understand what I'd done wrong, he futilely called out for the girl to come and handle the aforementioned unmentionables. Finally he wrapped the offending items in paper himself, with such a scandalised look on his face that I found it hard not to laugh.

These days I look forward to shopping for underwear because I never know what to expect. It makes no sense that I can confidently let a man at the markets tell me what bra size I should wear, in a country where I'm told I shouldn't sit next to an unrelated man on a long distance bus trip because I risk damaging my reputation. Whatever the logic, whether I go to an upmarket store staffed by open-minded women with a hands-on attitude, or to a small shop staffed by the local version of the morality police, I always come home having learnt something new about this fascinating and sometimes confusing country where I choose to live.

The First Cut is the Deepest - Sünnet

Whether you support it or not, the touchy subject of circumcision, or *sünnet* as it's called in Turkish, is one that can't be avoided if you stay in the country for any period of time. On my first trip here in 1990 I listened with baited breath as a fellow traveller, an Englishman called Adrian who was bicycling to India, told me about a ceremony he'd attended. Apparently the boys usually have a *kirve,* the Turkish equivalent of a male 'godparent' to help them. The father of the boy decided that as the guest of honour Adrian should take on this role and more. He held out a rusty razor blade to the hapless foreigner, and repeatedly urged him to do the deed. Adrian somehow managed to get out of performing the task itself, but it was a close thing.

Fast forward twenty odd years later to when I gave English lessons to the son of a woman who worked at my bank. The lessons always took place in their home and one day I arrived to learn her son had recently been circumcised. He was about eleven years old at the time and had no qualms about explaining the procedure to me in detail. Feeling weak I could only comment faintly that it must have hurt, a lot. He strongly denied this and to emphasise his point he proudly and firmly knocked on the protective box he was wearing. I felt extremely uncomfortable talking about it but I was the only one embarrassed by the subject.

Turks usually defer male circumcision until after the age of seven, and rather than being a private undertaking it is a very public coming-of-age ritual. The celebration is normally held after school closes for the summer holidays or in the autumn, just before school goes back. A boy who is to be circumcised is called *sünnet çocuğu*, child of the circumcision, and he is treated like a prince. Traditionally his father would buy him an elaborate circumcision outfit as well as clothes for their relatives to wear. The boy's costume consists of a satin cloak, often edged with feather boa finery in the same colour, a natty bow tie, an elaborate cummerbund, a *sünnet* sceptre and a matching hat. Some even get to wear an ornamental dagger tucked into their belt. A sash with the inscription *Maşallah,* meaning "May God protect the wearer from the evil eye", is worn across the body. The belief in the power of the evil eye, a curse believed to be cast by a malevolent glare known as *nazar* in Turkish, remains strong throughout the country.

These days the boy's costume can also be rented. Every town and city has at least one store specialising in *sünnet* clothing and accessories, although the market has also moved online with numerous companies investing in websites offering a richly seductive selection of outfits with exotic names like 'The Taj Mahal" or the 'Istanbul Silver White'.

Traditionally, a few days before the circumcision ceremony the boy visits his relatives and neighbors in his circumcision outfit and kisses the back of their hand before touching it to his forehead as a sign of respect. Every person whose hand is kissed customarily gives him money. In villages in Anatolia, the young boy, before being circumcised, travels on horseback or in a procession consisting of cars in and around the village. The boy is brought into the circumcision hall just before noon and won't dismount from his horse or get out of the car until he receives money from his father. Common to both rural and urban ceremonies is that all the guests come together and chant a *mevlit,* a special series of prayers, and eat a meal while waiting for the arrival of the little prince. When I lived in Kayseri in central Turkey local television stations would broadcast these events live. My husband and I liked to watch and comment on the proceedings while eating our dinner on freezing cold winter nights.

Much of these televised events consisted of watching people sitting around doing nothing more than eating and chatting. The camera would pan achingly slowly around the room, lingering on each and every table of guests in turn, before finally focussing on the guest of honour. Resplendent in his *sünnet* suit, the boy reclined on a double bed that was equally splendid. Positioned on a stage to give maximum exposure, the bed was dressed in special satin sheets with matching *sünnet* pillows. There might be towel beside him with his name and the date embroidered on it in gold or silver thread, commemorating the event. As he lay there smiling bravely his family and then all the relatives and other guests would come up one by one to give him a gift. It's usual to give a *Cumhuriyet Altını*, a gold coin of particular value, or a watch as a gift to the boy, in accordance to one's relationship with him or his parents. The handing over of presents is accompanied by the uttering of phrases such as *"Oldu da bitti Maşallah"*. "Well, it's all over and done" or *"Allahü ekber"*, "God is the greatest", to signal the end of the procedure and mark its importance.

Snug in our little apartment Kim and I would laugh at the accompanying advertisements for chocolate featuring little boys dressed in their *sünnet* prince finery. One commercial which always made us laugh showed the parents and all the relatives waiting in a large ornate room while a group of little boys searched desperately for a way out of the building. Before they could make good their escape they fell for the charms of a pretty ringleted little girl holding out a bar of a popular brand of chocolate. Unwittingly they allowed her to lure them to where their families were waiting, alongside the lavishly decorated beds in which they would rest and recline after the incision, receiving compliments and gifts. It was a clever take on an old tradition but elsewhere the fate of boys trying to get out of being circumcised was less amusing. As the celebration is costly, in families with more than one son it's common to wait until there's enough money to put both children through the procedure at the same time to save on expenses. Younger boys are excited by the prospect of getting presents but often older boys are all too aware of the pain they will suffer. I read of one instance in the south east of the country where a boy climbed onto the roof of a large outbuilding to hide, only to plunge to his death when a brittle tile gave way.

In big cities the procedure itself is frequently carried out in the sterile privacy of a hospital clinic. The boy might still dress up in his prince suit and ride a horse through the streets, but it can be many months after the event. In Istanbul, it is common to take the little boys to Eyüp Sultan

Mosque in the Golden Horn Suburb of Eyüp. This mosque is home to Istanbul's most holy shrine, believed to be the burial place of Ebu Eyüp el-Ensari, the standard-bearer to the Prophet Mohammed. Although the current mosque was built in 1800, the tomb dates back to 1458. Parents take their boys to visit the shrine and pray before the procedure and ensuing celebrations.

While *sünnet* is expensive, lack of funds is no reason for a boy to miss out. Local councils offer free circumcisions for boys from poor families, advertising the date by which they must register on huge billboards that go up in early spring. Some councils like to promote their largesse by rewarding the newly crowned kings and their families with boat trips along the Bosphorus to celebrate their entry into manhood. The happy recipients and their grateful parents are then dutifully photographed and their stories appear in the papers.

Whatever your opinion on the subject of circumcision, without it a Muslim boy can never be considered a man in Turkey. The tradition of *sünnet* seems to intrigue and repel foreigners in equal measures. Once when I was in Ankara with my father at *Anıt Kabır,* the huge mausoleum built to honour Atatürk, I ran after a little boy making a *sünnet* visit to ask if Dad could take his picture. Dad was completely enamoured by the idea of boys dressed up like little princes and I didn't have the heart to tell him until afterwards why the boy was dressed that way. I'm just thankful that unlike those undergoing the procedure, other than that one time in Ankara, the closest I've ever come to a *sünnet* ceremony is on television.

Antique Street

For as long as I can remember, Tellalzade Sokak in Kadıköy on the Asian side of Istanbul, has never been referred to by its registered name. Streets in Turkey are called after a person who once lived there and gave the street its identity, or for the trades carried out in the shops lining the road. Judging by the use of both a front vowel and a back vowel in the same word, that is an *'e'* with an *'a'*, *tellal* likely originates from Ottoman Turkish. Its primary definition is town crier. Combined with the word *zade* it means 'son of the town crier' and suggests this was where one lived. However this narrow street, walled in by the faded glory of smart apartment blocks from the 1960s, and more traditional brick and render *konak* houses tucked in side-by-side has always been designated as *Antik Sokak*, or Antique Street.

Maybe this is because a secondary meaning of *tellal* is 'broker'. The proprietors of the shops in Antique Street act as middlemen for the *eskici,* the sellers of old wares who roam the surrounding neighbourhoods, buying items no longer needed by their owners. After acquiring them for a few lira they bring them here in search of a quick profit. Once inside the doors of the antique stores these unwanted belongings are reinvented and offered for sale as much sought after and cherished treasures.

Even though I don't need anything I like to browse through the objects for sale in *Antik Sokak* and often have a light snack at the *Esnaf lokantası*, a kind of tradesmen's canteen located near the corner. I've been to many such eateries throughout Turkey, and they always have one hearty staple meal which they produce every day, supplemented by an assortment of dishes that change according to the mood of the cook and what's in season. Aimed at working men, these establishments offer nutritious and tasty food at reasonable prices. Girls from respectable families are often warned against eating in such places as to do so will instantly render them lower class, but being foreign and a fan of this simple but tasty fare I have no such inhibitions.

The one in *Antik Sokak* specialises in *nohutlu tavuklu pilav,* rice served with chicken and chickpeas. I first ate this dish in the mishmash of streets around Eminönü, a wholesale centre that fans out from the perimeters of the *Kapalı Çarşı*, the famous Grand Bazaar, which reaches all the way to the shores of the Golden Horn. Back then servings of chicken and chickpeas were sold by men pushing carts made from the base of old-fashioned prams, with a rectangular glass display case haphazardly secured on top. Behind the steaming panes a mountain of rice glistened from the butter in which it was cooked. A generous scoop was tapped out onto an aluminium plate, adorned with strips of boiled shredded chicken and then dotted with chickpeas. I always added a liberal helping of *pul biber*, dried chilli flakes, and a pinch of salt.

In Antique Street most of the customers of the tradesman's café are dealers from the shops in the street, as well as shop assistants from surrounding ones, such as Fish and Migros Supermarket Streets. They do a brisk business as the area transforms from a cheap student hang to a more upmarket shopping area, which has seen similar eateries forced to close in the face of rising rents. Inside, single men sit at laminex tables assiduously wiped clean by the young trainee waiter who can't take his eyes off me, the only woman in the place. Reluctantly he tears himself away from my exotic and therefore captivating blue eyes to walk deliveries of food, on plates well covered in plastic wrap with cutlery on the side, to nearby offices. I fill my fork with rice, chicken and chickpeas and slowly chew in time with the old Turkish song being played on an ancient portable radio hanging above the service counter.

More often these days, the young and the restless, students and those who claim the profession of official protestors against anything and everything fill the street on hot summer nights. They sit on traditional low woven straw stools grouped around equally small tables, each with its own basil plant, a beaten copper polished lidded bowl holding sugar and a heavily stained aluminium ashtray. Above them a picturesquely large untamed grape vine is trained over the roll out of canopies and cables strung across the street. The number of tea houses has proliferated of late, and they cluster together at either end of the street.

This growth in the number of people frequenting the street has been matched by an increase and variety in the type of businesses in operation. In the past there were only one or two quality antique dealers flanked by numerous junk shops, including one piled so high with detritus you couldn't pass much beyond the entryway. Nowadays more shops have opened, displaying high end products such as ruby glass, enamel plated cigarette cases from the early days of the Turkish Republic and exquisite furniture inlaid with minutely detailed mother-of-pearl in their windows, hoping to tempt the increasing number of foreign tourists making day trips to this side of Istanbul. One or two junk stores remain, but most have been replaced by specialty stores selling multiple versions of the one thing, be it records, gramophones or vintage stereo systems. Dotted between the shops new cafes have opened up, specialising in Italian coffee or doubling as art galleries. These serve to call attention to discrete long established restaurants, including one I used to frequent. Run more like a private club, I went there once a week to engage in a Turkish English language exchange group. There are no community centres or halls for rent in Istanbul, so groups of likeminded individuals often approach café owners and negotiate use of the premises on the understanding a certain amount of food and drink will be consumed and paid for. On other nights tango classes were held beneath the ferns hanging from the sheets of clear plastic roofing enclosing the back garden, while the sound of Turkish folk music sung by friends of twenty years standing drifted down from the burgundy painted rooms upstairs. On Friday and Saturday nights the owners prepared special menus offering a rich array of Turkish *meze*. Most usually translated as entrees or *hors d'oeuvre*, *meze* consist of small servings of food, such as cheese, melon, grilled eggplant or capsicum and sundry other savoury delights, designed to be consumed while partaking in *rakı*. *Rakı*, or lion's milk as the locals like to call it, is Turkey's national alcoholic drink made from anise. However it is not just a drink. It is an aid to memory, a symbol of the past and a panacea for life's woes.

At first glance Tellalzade Sokak looks similar to other streets found in any number of cities around the world. Yet beneath the uniform veneer of luxury antiques and quiet order is a neighbourhood made up of a vibrant mix of people of discordant political persuasions and interests. Much like the locals in other cities and towns of Istanbul and Turkey, the inhabitants are united by their love of laughter, passionate argument, food and dance.

Metrobus Dreams

People who live in Istanbul will be amused and even laugh out loud as they read this, but when I catch the Istanbul metrobus from Soğutluçeşme in Kadıköy to Zincirlikuyu on the other side of the Bosphorus, I am transported to a different world. The complete route covers a total of fifty kilometres and the long bendy buses carry nearly a million people a day from one end of Istanbul to the other. Passengers ordinarily describe their trips as jam-packed, too hot and often smelly, but to me the journeys on these crowded vehicles are an adventure where every stop brings me to another time and place.

We start in *Söğütlüçeşme*, a name which conjures up visions of a refreshing fountain shaded by willows. I imagine the neighbourhood women walking there every morning to collect the water they need for daily use. While their husbands think they are being dutiful wives, I see them gathered around the fountain, chatting and relaxing and catching up on the news as their children play and run circles around them. As the women gossip they surreptitiously eye off any unmarried daughters to see who would be a good match for their sons. The girls in question walk slowly to and from the fountain, dawdling when they come to particular houses in the hope of attracting the attention of the boy they fancy. In the past they might have looked for a chance to leave a chickpea or another such coded item on the path for the boy to find. I don't remember the exact meaning of leaving a chickpea, but I know the chickpeas widely grown in the Mediterranean are thought to have come from Afghanistan. They are called *kabuli* in Hindi and Urdu, which in Turkish means 'acceptance'.

Next we come to *Fikirtepe*, which roughly means the 'hill of ideas'. As we move slowly down the side of the valley and stop to take on more passengers, I stare out through the tinted windows and wonder what deep and brilliant thoughts once emanated from this place. In 1876 a wooden hunting lodge was built here for Sultan Murad V. His reign came to end after only three months due to his declining mental state so I think it's unlikely it was named for him. He was brought up within the confines of the *kafes* in Topkapı Palace. Known as the 'cage' in English, the *kafes* was a two storey building in the palace grounds where the heirs to the empire were kept locked away until they ascended the throne or died. Elaborately appointed, the *kafes* provided all the luxuries a prince could want, except for windows on the ground floor and freedom.

Now all that is left of the suburb's possibly brilliant past is a ramshackle *hamam*, or Turkish bath, on the edge of a desolate wasteland awaiting urban renewal. For many years the area was home to Turks who migrated from the south east during the country's internal turbulence of the 1980s and 1990s. They lived in ramshackle huts called *gecekondu*, which literally translates as 'night dwelling'. Newly arrived residents collected old pieces of wood, scraps of corrugated iron and even flattened oil cans and hastily put together shelters before the sun came up. At the time a law existed that deemed any dwelling erected overnight legal, but didn't stipulate as to their quality. The haphazardly built apartment blocks which later replaced the *gecekondu* have since been declared unsafe, and the inhabitants forced to move elsewhere in their search for a better life.

At *Uzunçayır*, I envisage the long fields to which the name refers. Fully grown sheep and brilliantly white newborn lambs dot meadows covered with long blades of grass swaying gently in the cooling breezes. In my mind's eye the reality of the ugly sprawling mess of over and underpasses connecting the intersection of two major highways and numerous side roads is always blanketed with the red poppies of spring or the purity of winter snow.

It's hard to believe now but not that long ago much of this side of Istanbul was a wilderness of green. Densely packed forests boasting a rich array of wildlife provided a cool respite for the sultans and their court during the gruelling heat of summer while the lush pastures bred succulent lambs for their feasts.

After a slow crawl out of the basin comes *Acıbadem,* which is also the name of my favourite Turkish almond meal biscuit. The name correctly translated means 'bitter almond' but is a misnomer for these moistly sweet treats. Caught up in the delight of remembering the taste, I wonder if the *acıbadem* on the metrobus line is a sobriquet. Was this the site of true love turned bad, when a man's little almond blossom turned out to be a bruised and damaged flower? Or is the story more mundane, and the soil only yielded almond trees whose fruit was bitter to the taste? I know from talking to local taxi drivers that the hills next to the highway we're on used to be covered in orchards. In spring the air would be heady with the scent of fruit blossoms. I try to finish the tale of the fragile bloom of my imagination but sadly, as I gaze out the bus windows my dream is interrupted by insistent lines of new villas cascading down the terraces, mowing down the remaining patches of unspoiled landscape.

The meaning of the word *Altunizade,* also the name of the next suburb on the route, is open to interpretation. *Altun* on its own means 'gold coloured', and *zade* derives from Ottoman Turkish and means 'son of'. The present day suburb sits on a hill that in the past would have had a commanding view to the Bosphorus away in the distance. I like to imagine *Altunizade* was the much awaited first born son of a pasha and his blushing bride. On reaching maturity a grand palace was built for him here and he lived out his days casting a golden light on the rolling hills of Istanbul. In reality the neighbourhood was in fact established by a pasha, one Altunizade Ismail Zühdi Pasha, in the second half of the nineteenth century. He was responsible for building a mosque, the main road, a *hamam* and other properties which he rented out. Numerous members of his family can still be found here, resting peacefully in the local cemetery. In my story his proud parents lie there too, alongside their beloved boy.

The next stop on the metrobus line is *Burhaniye Mahallesi. Burhan* in Ottoman Turkish means 'proof' or 'witness'. This small and almost hidden suburb sits tucked away high above the turbulent waters of the Bosphorus, on the edge of which Beylerbeyi Palace can be found. When I look out the bus window I can see the residents creeping down the hill to spy on the ladies of the palace. Were they privy to the secrets of the sultans? Did they watch as the courtesans, dressed in their finery, giggled and laughed as they waited for the arrival of a golden *caique* to come and row them to the Sweet Waters of Asia on balmy summer nights? Were the locals of Burhaniye the first to gossip about who had a new gentleman caller and who had fallen from grace?

The actual story behind the name is equally interesting but far less romantic. The neighbourhood was originally settled by refugees from the 1876 April Uprising in Bulgaria. First known as Muhacir Köyü, 'Immigrant village', it was renamed for the Burhaniye Mosque built in 1902 by Sultan Abdul Hamid II for his son Burhanettin Efendi. This story might be true but I still prefer my version.

The next stop, *Boğaziçi Köprüsü*, the Bosphorus Bridge, needs no imagining as the moment the metrobus starts the crossing one is swept away by the sun sparkling on the bright blue waters below and bouncing off the minarets that sketch in the skyline. As we cross the bridge wide brushstrokes of detail paint in the city and there is more than enough to feed my daydreams before I alight at *Zincirlikuyu*. Here, at the stop whose name means 'well or shaft equipped with a chain', my imagination halts as if suddenly tethered to the earth. I return once more to the present and alight from the bus to join the throng of commuters scurrying for the exits, heading off on more journeys to other places with equally mysterious and bewitching names.

Turkish Tombs – Dervish Traditions

One the quirky features I love about Istanbul are the tombs dedicated to *dede* or senior dervishes. A dervish is a member of a Muslim religious order who has taken vows of poverty and austerity. Most often associated with the Sufi religious order, there are various orders of dervishes in Turkey, such as the Mevlevi or Whirling Dervishes as they are known to tourists, and the lesser known Nakşibendis and Bektaşi dervish groups. Almost all of them trace their origins back to specific Muslim saints and teachers. Their tombs are always pale mint green in colour and located in odd places, such as in the garden of an apartment block or right in the middle of a path. No matter how inconvenient the location, Turkish people believe it is bad luck to move them.

There are many such tombs in unexpected places in Istanbul, but I have two favourites. The first is probably the better known, because it is located amongst the railway lines of Haydarpaşa Railway Station. Built in 1909 on the Asian side of Istanbul by the Anatolian Railway, Haydarpaşa was the terminus for the Baghdad and Hedjaz railways. Two German architects, Otto Ritter and Helmut Conu, were hired to design the new building. They chose a

Neo-classical structure, and German and Italian stonemasons crafted the embellishments on the facade of the terminal. A small German neighbourhood in the nearby Yeldeğirmeni quarter of Kadıköy was established to house the engineers and craftsmen who worked on the project.

Many Turks worked on the project too, and when plans were drawn up to lay the tracks a decision was made to move the tomb of Haydar Baba. Buharalı Haydar Dede, to give him his full name, was the head or sheik of a Nakşibendi lodge, and is believed to have died around 1700 AD. It's rumoured that the night before the work was due to start the supervisor of the works had a dream. Haydar Baba appeared before him and said it would make him uncomfortable if they moved his grave. Shaken but undeterred the supervisor shrugged off his unease and went back to work the next day. However the following night Haydar Baba came to the supervisor again and repeated his statement more forcefully this time, placing his hands around the supervisor's throat and squeezing tightly. Naturally afraid, the supervisor called a halt to the work and had the new lines laid on either side of the tomb, leaving Haydar Baba undisturbed.

The second tomb I love is in a suburb called Merdivenköy, also on the Asian side of Istanbul. Today this is a heavily built up residential area but the suffix *köy*, meaning 'village', points to its history. During the reign of the Ottoman sultans the palace was supplied with milk, cheese and yoghurt from dairies operating in Merdivenköy. In the past, there was also a dervish order of which the Ottoman Sultan Beyazit I, nicknamed 'lightening', was a member. He laid siege to the city of Constantinople in the late fourteenth century, holding it to ransom until defeated by Timur, known as Tamerlane in English, the Central Asian conqueror. Later on Beyazit was martyred on the Ziverbey road, modern day Minibus Street, at Çemenzar, a suburb that abuts Merdivenköy.

The Ottomans had also called Beyazit '*gözcü baba*', the 'watchman' or 'lookout', meaning the one who spied on the Byzantines. More generally it is the name given to a person who watches over the city, in honour of their past deeds. Beyazit is believed to have been interred in a grave marked with cypresses, next to a sacred spring, on a hill called Namazgah. No such grave remains today but a part of the Merdivenköy neighbourhood continues to be referred to as Gözcubaba.

Today, a stand of cypresses still exists at the intersection which marks the boundary of Gözcubaba and Merdivenköy. On the low wall surrounding them a marble slab, inscribed with Ottoman Turkish marks the spot. I had a friend ask their Ottoman language teacher to translate the inscription on the stone. It reads, "This hall was built 1308 years after *hijra*, dervish born Hilmi Dede". Hilmi Dede was a Bektaşi in 1842 in the Göngörmez neighbourhood of Istanbul, close to Sultanahmet. Records show he was posted to the Istanbul Sultan Şahkulu Dervish lodge in Merdivenköy in 1864 and spent the ensuing years developing it. *Hijra* is the journey of the prophet Muhammad and his followers from Mecca to Medina. It is used to set the first day of the Islamic calendar and roughly corresponds to July 622 in the Georgian calendar. According to the tabular Islamic calendar 1308 years after *hijra* would have been 1891 AD. I take this to mean that Hilmi Dede was instrumental in founding a lodge or hall, called *sofa* in Turkish, meaning a long room with rooms opening on to it, on this spot at that time. When he died in 1907 he was buried in the winter courtyard of the dervish lodge and later on his relatives built a special garden in his memory in Gözcubaba.

My other favourite tomb is just down the hill from this spot. It is ringed by a green fence, and sits in the middle of a busy road feeding onto a major highway. In order to reach it I had to dash across the road while looking madly in all directions because no one obeys traffic rules in Istanbul. Another pedestrian took advantage of my courage to make the crossing too. Unlike me she had come to pray and immediately entered the enclosure to begin her supplications.

This tomb is dedicated to two dervishes, Gül Baba and Mah Baba. The first name is well known in history. Originally named Cafer, Gül Baba was an Ottoman Bektaşi dervish poet who was a close companion of Sultan Süleyman the Magnificent. Originally from a village in Sivas in the north east of the country, Gül Baba is thought to have died in Buda, Hungary, during the first Muslim religious ceremony held there after the Ottoman victory in 1541. Others believe he was killed during fighting below the walls of the city on the twenty first of August in the same year. Regardless of the circumstances under which he lost his life, Süleyman declared Gül Baba patron saint of the city and is believed to have been one of his coffin bearers.

His actual burial site is in an octagonal *türbe* in Mescet Street in Budapest. The tomb was converted into a Roman Catholic chapel in the seventeenth century but was still accessible to Muslim pilgrims until the nineteenth century.

Then, in 1885, the Ottoman government commissioned a Hungarian engineer to restore it. When the work was completed in 1914, it was declared a national monument. The site was restored again in the 1960s and the 1990s and is now the property of the Republic of Turkey.

I could find no information about Mah Baba, and the little information I did find out that is specific to this particular tomb in Istanbul comes from İsmail Tosun Saral, a writer and expert on Turkish Hungarian relations. He writes that another Gül Baba lies here, on the right hand side of the road from Merdivenköy to Üçgöztepe. Saral quotes from Dr Bedri Noyan Dedebaba, himself a respected dervish and researcher of Alevi and Bektaşi history, who states this Gül Baba died in a battle between the Ottoman Turks and the Byzantines in June of the year 1329 on the Gregorian calendar.

Whatever the real story behind this tomb, I know the woman praying to Gül Baba and Mah Baba believed her wishes would come true. Her faith is as strong as that of Istanbul residents who believe the resting place of a saint should be left in its original location no matter what. Although Istanbul is a city undergoing rapid urban development these tombs and the beliefs they represent stand as a testament to the way progress continues to bend to tradition in Turkey.

.

A Long Way from Home

Tucked away on the slopes up behind the port of Harem on the Asian side of Istanbul, almost hidden by heavy containers and giant cranes, is the little visited Haydarpaşa Cemetery. Dating back to 1855 when the Turkish Government gave the site to the British Government, it contains about six thousand graves of victims of the Crimean War. Sadly, the majority of those buried here died as a result of a cholera epidemic raging through Istanbul then, rather than directly from wounds sustained in battle. Many of the cholera victims came from the nearby Selimiye Barracks, known to the West from the work of the 'Lady with the Lamp', better known as Florence Nightingale. Her calming presence was heralded by the warm glow of the lamp she always carried as she went from bed to bed tending to the many wounded and dying soldiers.

Twelve years later, British civilian burials were also allowed in this site. During the First World War the Turks used the cemetery for the interment of Commonwealth Prisoners of War. Then, after Armistice was declared and Istanbul was occupied by allied troops from 1918 until 1923, further burials of foreigners occurred in the grounds.

The day I visited the cemetery it was bitterly cold. The punishing gusts of the *poyraz*, a winter wind that blows down from the Black Sea, added to the already sombre and melancholy air of the cemetery. This wind takes its name from Boreas, the Ancient Greek northern wind god, and he seemed particularly angry that day. We were met at the ramshackle gate by the caretaker, a smiling unshaven man who greeted us briefly before returning to the task of feeding the chickens which had run around the back of his small one storey house on our arrival.

Turning left, we began to walk towards a gentle slope of vivid green lawn unrolling as smoothly as a carpet. Headstones marking the graves, a ghostly white in colour, were planted a respectful distance from each other. They were guarded by tall trees pruned to grow into heavily stylised forms. The absence of foliage made their bare limbs stand out in sharp relief against the grey of the sky. When the branches rasped sharply against each other it sounded as though they were deliberately screeching in time with the noise of the wind.

We passed many graves marking the final resting place of captains, lieutenants and infantrymen who'd died in the Crimea. They are uniform in style and predominantly commemorate the inhabitants as soldiers and loyal subjects rather. Alongside the graves of these military casualties are the much more personal ones belonging to civilians. Some of them, the smaller ones, contain the memories of a much loved only child or even all the children from the one family. The majority were the sons and daughters of government diplomats posted to a foreign consulate in Pera, the Western name for Beyoğlu, on the European side of the city. They too died as a result of epidemics randomly sweeping through Istanbul. The Christian symbol of the lamb, signifying purity and innocence, often features on their stones.

Certain graves, such as that of Arthur and Rhodie Tully, immediately catch the eye for the emotion they express. Mr and Mrs Tully were laid to rest side-by-side, their two souls connected through carved marble hearts, reflecting their love for one another and for God, their courage and intelligence, and of course, their mortality. The only reference I can find to this couple is to Rhodie, who was a champion of the abilities of Ottoman women to work as clerks. In the nineteenth century only non-Turkish women were allowed to work in offices.

Other graves stand out due to the historical curiosity of the occupant. One of these is that of Marian Langiewicz, a Polish patriot who was a military leader in the Polish

January Uprising against the Russians in 1863. After declaring himself a dictator and trying to set up a government he was defeated and jailed. After his release he lived in Switzerland for a time before coming to Turkey and entering the Turkish service where he was known as 'Langie Bey'. He died in 1887.

The cemetery also honours other non-British citizens who fought in the First World War. It contains the graves of nearly one hundred and fifty Hindu, Muslim and Sikh soldiers of the Indian Army who died as Prisoners of War (POWs) as a result of their participation in the Mesopotamia campaign, in what is now modern-day Iraq. They are generally known as *sepoys*, and were Indian soldiers serving under British or other European orders. Over the course of the many campaigns on this front, close to 675,000 Indian fighting troops as well as hundreds of thousands of auxiliary troops were involved in Mesopotamia. When General Townshend's troops surrendered in April 1916, the POWs were marched all the way from Mesopotamia to POW camps in Turkey. It is believed those who survived were held in camps in the town of Afyonkarahisar, so named for the poppies grown there under the watchful guard of a black fortress atop a craggy hill.

These men were originally laid to rest in Mashlak and Osmanieh Muslim Cemeteries. In 1961 when these cemeteries could no longer be maintained, their remains were moved to Haydarpaşa Cemetery. The ashes of the Hindus, whose remains were cremated in accordance with their faith, were scattered near the memorial commemorating their service, while their comrades of Muslim faith were re-interred here. Under Islam the deceased must be buried because Muslims believe the dead must be treated with the same respect as the living. This belief originates from the Prophet Mohammed's statement that breaking the bones of the deceased's body is like breaking them in life. Burning the dead for cremation, like breaking the bones of the dead or other such mutilation, is therefore prohibited, as is accepting or encouraging such treatment, unless a large number of people have died as the result of a contagious disease.

The grave that intrigued me the most was that of a Captain H. E. Smith of the Ship Chalmers. He died in June 1855 so he could have been a victim of cholera. However his grave is in a shaded grove down a gentle slope, set well away from those of the other foreigners. It's almost obscured by overhanging branches, and looks dirty and neglected. Curiously, the tombstone is a Muslim one, and carved with flowers rather than topped with a turban as would be usual for the grave of a man. However the inscription is a Christian one and reads, "The lord gave and the Lord hath taken'. I have to wonder why he is lying in a corner on his own. Why is his grave not a traditional Christian one? Maybe he was a convert or preferred the company of Turks and so was shunned by his own kind. Perhaps the gravestone was chosen by his Turkish love who hoped one day to be laid to rest beside the man she loved.

Whatever the story behind the life and death of Captain Smith, like all those who spend eternity in the grounds of Haydarpaşa Cemetery, he died a long way from home.

An Hour of Your Time – Turkish Death Rituals

A Turkish friend recently invited me to attend a *mevlit* to be held for her mother. Her mum had been failing for months, going from being a chirpy chatty woman to a small silent figure swaddled in a now too large bed, who no longer spoke but always smiled when she saw her darling Meral.

I felt honoured to be asked but also a bit nervous and uncertain. I had once visited the family of a Turkish friend who'd died, but never been part of a formal ceremony. All I knew was that a *mevlit* is a series of prayers said at various times during a person's life and death but I didn't know how I would be expected to behave. My participation was as a friend of the family, not as a foreigner, so I didn't think it was right to ask Meral what I should do. Also, remembering the awkwardness of my Turkish friends over how to treat me when I returned to Istanbul after the death of my father, I didn't like to ask any of them what I should do either.

I arrived at the appointed time and day to find my friend's salon full of family and friends, mainly people I didn't know. Taking a deep breath I made my way into the room. Over near the couches a young man was setting up cables leading to the apartment below, where Meral's mother had lived. As I watched him curiously Meral came up behind me from the kitchen and greeted me warmly with a kiss on either cheek, before taking me downstairs to hang my coat. She told me that the *hafiz,* the person who would read the Koran, was going to sit upstairs in her apartment. The cables were necessary to connect speakers placed in her mother's apartment so the rest of the mourners could follow the prayers.

Back upstairs I went out onto the balcony to pay my respects to Meral's husband. He introduced me to various male relatives who'd flown over from Europe. After a few minutes of small talk I wandered back inside to wait and see what would happen. A tiny old woman urged me to sit down and within moments a plate, piled high with food, was presented to me. I took it along with the lemon sherbet drink I was offered. Not wanting to offend I ate a few bites but was relieved to see other people were also making only token efforts with the food. I was still trying to balance my plate and glass when a large well-dressed man appeared, flanked by two younger men. I was told by a woman sitting on my left that he was the *imam,* the spiritual leader of the local mosque, and had come to say the prayers.

Within minutes plates and glasses were whisked away, people who'd been smoking on the balcony came inside and everywhere I looked women were removing headscarves from their handbags. I'd come prepared, so I put mine on too. As soon as the recitation started I began to examine the people around me. Predominantly women, they ranged from the very old to those in their early twenties. There were no children present. All in attendance were elegantly attired in stylish contemporary clothes, reflecting the background of the family. Only a few of the women wore makeup and discrete pieces of jewellery and the one who wore the most, dressed as if for an evening out, spent a lot of her time worrying about her headscarf slipping off. It was made of fine silk and thus was more fashionable then practical. Opposite her another woman, dressed modestly in a long skirt and loose top, mouthed all the words along with the *hafiz*. Her eyes were closed and she swayed slightly in time with the verses. When certain actions were called for, such as wiping the sides of the faces with both hands, starting at the forehead and working towards the chin*, the made up woman took care not to

* At the end of prayers, participants recite the Fatiha (the opening verse of the Koran) and then wipe their face. In essence, when a prayer is finished the devotee washes their face with the blessings of the prayers.

touch her skin while the second woman firmly made contact. I told a friend about this later and she expressed surprise that any of the women were wearing any makeup or jewellery at all. I learnt too late that it was tradition to attend clean-faced and had to hope my bright lipstick had been forgiven as the ignorance and not the insult of a foreigner.

The ceremony lasted about an hour and I can't honestly say I understood very much of the *mevlit* although I looked it up later and now know it is a long poem about the life of the Prophet celebrating his birth. During the recitation I used the time to reflect on my life, the loss of my father and my place in this sometimes alien culture. In contrast to me the rest of the mourners participated in the *mevlit* with such ease it seemed as though their bodies had been trained from birth to speak the language of prayer.

After farewelling Meral with the set phrase of condolence, *'Başınız sağ olsun'*, I rejoined the sunny world of the living outside. Back home, as is my wont, I started to research what I had experienced, painstakingly translating websites written in Turkish to try to get the most accurate descriptions. I learnt that according to Islam the reading of the Koran from start to finish, called *hatim-ıskat,* should occur as close to seven days after the death as possible.

Ideally it takes place after settling the debts of the deceased, giving away their clothes, and settling on alms to be distributed to the poor. There is a lot more to be done but what I find most interesting is that there are clearly specified actions governed by detailed rules to cover every different scenario. When my father died I remember floundering after the funeral service, as I had no idea what to do or how to live with such an enormous loss. The grief associated with the death of a loved one is devastating, and while I'm not religious, I think following religious strictures at times like these must be comforting.

The People You Meet

In my many years of living and travelling through Turkey, I've met a lot of different people, all of whom called themselves Turks. However what they mean by this depends on their individual circumstances, the specific variants linked to their familial history and other almost indefinable elements of their identity. Being Turkish is a curious blend of the past and the present in fluctuating measures, and nowhere is this better illustrated than in Istanbul, the famed city of seven hills. People in Turkey move vast distances away from their families, for work, study or marriage. Some are poor and illiterate yet can tell you more about the Urartian history of their tiny village than a trained academic, while others are startlingly rich and cultured and able to trace their roots back to Ottoman times. All of them weave stories of their past, usually connected to their home town, into their present, resulting in a rich mix of difference. As a result, while these hills might be home to a population of nearly twenty million people collectively known as Turks, there is no single definitive narrative of Turkish culture.

Istanbul is best seen as a series of interconnected villages whose inhabitants speak a similar language but with dialectic markers which refer to their specific local cultures and traditions. Where a Turk identifies as being from, who their parents and grandparents were, the way they practice religion and the effect these factors have on their world view and daily practices, as well as the way they use language to describe the world as they see it, all influence and create these multiple manifestations of Turkish culture. Linking all these versions of being Turkish is the strong connection Turks maintain with the people and the place of their birth, both literally and figuratively.

Back in the mid-1990s, Nevşehir in central Turkey was a small country town and remains the closest 'big' town to a number of small outlying villages. Although only twenty minutes away by *dolmuş* or shared taxi from Göreme, one of the major tourist villages in Cappadocia, Nevşehir has none of the natural beauty associated with the area. It is decidedly without the glamour of Istanbul as the local shops cater to no one other than the local farmers. There are rows of shops selling all the same things, mainly harnesses, leather straps, metal objects such as hooks, blades, and other pieces of farming equipment I didn't recognize. If you can't get what you need from the huge weekly market or from one of the pokey stores located in the maze of streets and laneways leading off the main street, then you don't need it. It was here that my husband Kim and I found ourselves wandering around one day, trying to buy some writing paper. The internet was still in its infancy then, and we were travelling around Europe for six months. Every major stop on our trip was marked by its *poste restante* address, and I was a faithful correspondent.

Eventually we found ourselves in a typical Turkish stationery shop. It was packed to the ceiling on one side with school notebooks, small writing pads, diaries, reams of paper, colorful cardboard, books of coloured paper, drawing paper, small canvases, sketch blocks, clear and patterned plastic contact, brown paper, cellophane, ornate wrapping paper, and old postcards. On the other side there were boxes of erasers, pencils, pens, paints, crayons, Textas, markers and rulers, games, toys, and plastic musical instruments. Then there were the stickers, vibrant butterflies, silver motorbikes, every animal species ever known to roam the earth, pink princesses drowning in tulle, in short, more types of stickers than I knew existed. The owner spoke some English and after asking us the usual questions of "Where are you from?" and "Do you like Turkey?" he left us alone to ponder over which writing paper we would buy.

Would I buy the lonely sweetheart writing paper imprinted with bouquets of roses trailing down the side of each leaf, or the more masculine set with the soldier dressed in fatigues complete with machine gun printed on the right hand corner of every page? I imagined a lonely soldier on duty out in the east, alone save for a flock of sheep nearby, pining for his girl. Would his heart leap on receipt of a floral envelope from back home, perhaps scented with rose water? Was the letter to be quickly hidden deep in a pocket to savour later, on his own, or did he open it straight away and succumb to his feelings of homesickness? This daydream was much easier to conjure up than one involving the camouflage paper so I quickly moved on to the rest of the selection. I was very tempted by one offering different profiles of Ataturk on each sheet, but in the end I settled for something that actually gave me enough room to write more than a few lines per page.

After we paid, the owner asked us if we'd ever been to Istanbul, where he usually lived. He was pleased to learn we were going there the following week and told us he played recorder for the Istanbul Symphony Orchestra. As it was summer he'd come back to his hometown to help his father out in the family shop. He did so every year he said, because much as he liked living in a big city, home was best. We were quick to say yes to his offer to hear him play. With no ceremony he launched into an old Anatolian folk song that spoke of hope mixed with longing and despair. Although I've long forgotten the man's name, I will always remember the haunting beauty of the music, and the almost joyous feeling of melancholy and nostalgia that washed over me as he played.

Some years later I was living in Istanbul and working at a private college teaching English. The school was located in an apartment building on Bağdat Caddesi, a street famous for businesses catering to the wealthy on the Asian side of Istanbul. It was owned by an unscrupulous man with a myriad of connections to the military and large pharmaceutical companies with big staff training budgets. Most of my students came from the same companies and I taught them in evening classes, but I had one morning class of all women. They were mainly well-to-do mothers wanting to help their school age children succeed and get a good place at university.

Duygu was an *Istanbullu*, someone who was born and bred in Istanbul. At fifty six she had the heart of a teenager and the mischievous nature of a small child. It was her heart's desire to dance with Ricky Martin, but she told me that she couldn't take dance lessons because the neighbours would gossip. She was learning English because her daughter and granddaughter lived in England, and she wanted to make sure she would always be able to talk to her newest granddaughter Çiçek, her delicate little flower.

Duygu had grown up in the area, but said Istanbul was a vastly different city from the one of her childhood. She spent her early years by the water at Erenköy, playing hide and seek in the trees and staying out late on the beach until her mother called her from their house on Bağdat Caddesi to come home and eat. This would be impossible to do today. A modernisation project to reclaim the waterfront was completed in the 1980s and the beaches where Duygu used to play are now lost under Sahil Yolu, a major road leading all the way up the coast to Bostancı and beyond. At some points along the coast it's now a ten minute walk back up to Bağdat Caddesi so you'd need a loudspeaker to call your children home. Apartment blocks built around the time of Duygu's childhood still dot the coastline and make up some of the most expensive real estate on this side of the Sea of Marmara.

One day my morning class was talking about the tradition of the Turkish bath. I hadn't been to one at that stage, and was more than happy to divert from our scheduled grammar lesson while the women talked. Duygu told of going to a *hamam* with her grandmother. She thought it was when she was quite young, maybe only about three or four years old. Her grandmother wore all her usual jewellery, including diamond bracelets with matching earrings and smaller diamonds in her hair. The chief *hamam* woman came into the bath and carefully helped her grandmother take off all her baubles which were then placed in a lacquered wooden box and securely locked.

Her grandmother always took her own bathing equipment to the *hamam*. Duygu remembers the *hamam tası,* the bowls for scooping up and pouring water over the body, being gold or gold-plated. She said they were very heavy, and when she looked into them she could see a fish on the bottom with bright green emeralds for eyes. There were stone couches built around the sides of the *hamam*, covered with a special cloth they always brought with them. The best part, she told us, was that she and her grandmother would lie in there for hours talking and sweating and relaxing.

Duygu also had an aunt who owned a large *konak* house on the hill leading down from Sultanahmet, near the houses owned by the old money Köprülü family. Her aunt's house had a *hamam* in the basement, and the top floor was taken up by one large room used for entertaining guests. The family had a black servant, a large Negro* woman with a ring in her nose. This woman played a huge role in disciplining Duygu, as her mother and aunt frequently told her the servant would whisk her away from her family, never to return, if Duygu were bad. One day, all the women and servants of the household were engaged in cleaning the top room. First they removed all the Persian rugs from the floor, and took them outside to be beaten and aired. Underneath were squares of woven matting used to provide warmth which were also removed. The floor below was wood and had to be scrubbed with soap to clean it. After lunch, while all the grownups were otherwise engaged, Duygu created a new game for her brother to play with her. The soap for washing the floors was bought in bulk and kept in large sacks. Duygu discovered that if she rubbed it onto the wooden floor they could have endless fun sliding from one side of the room to the other. She and her brother did this for hours, only ceasing when the women came back to clean. When work started again there was a huge hullabaloo because all the soap Duygu had rubbed into the

*I am using the term 'Negro' because this is the word Duygu used.

floor, combined with what the women had added, resulted in gigantic waves of suds which took forever to wash away. Hearing the annoyance in the voices of the cleaning women, Duygu hid in a cupboard for hours in fear that her mother and aunt's threats would come true. When she was finally discovered any punishment was forgotten in the relief that she was all right.

Although thoroughly modern, Duygu was a bridge to the past. I had lunch with her at her home one day and met some of her friends. They were uniformly slim and tall, extremely glamorous women of a certain age who went skiing in Aspen every winter and had discrete plastic surgery as it became necessary to hold back time. We dined off old exquisite china and after the meal I took the opportunity to look more closely at the items displayed around the room. When I commented on an old book on a stand Duygu told me it was the nineteenth century family Koran bound between two hand-worked silver plates. Next to it was a silver bowl that was clearly very valuable. Duygu casually mentioned it had belonged to her great uncle who was the last Grand Vizier of Turkey. At the turn of the century he built a small apartment block in Laleli that boasted the first private elevator ever to be installed in the country. Like the life Duygu was born into, the building no longer exists.

Although more than fifteen years younger than Duygu, Aysun, another woman in my class, talked about the *Bayram* of her childhood with the same note of yearning wistfulness I heard when Duygu spoke of her childhood. *Bayram* is the Turkish word for festival but usually refers to special days connected to religious occasions. One important *Bayram* is the *Şeker Bayramı* or Sugar Festival, held to mark the end of the fasting month of Ramazan. After thirty days of neither drinking nor eating during daylight hours, this holiday is an orgy of chocolate consumption, where family visits family and close family friends. For three days business is suspended and the roads are clogged with people busily visiting relatives in order of age and importance. The youngest children kiss the hands of their elders and touch their hands to their foreheads as a sign of respect, all the while secretly hoping for a large coin in return.

For Aysun, a *Bayram* was not a holiday in the modern sense, nor was it solely to commemorate a religious event. The true meaning for the women in my morning English class was how *Bayram* reinforced family connections and ensured continuity. Yes, they all agreed with a smile, in the past, they received new clothes every *Bayram* but not like now. You didn't just go to the store to buy them, your mother or grandmothers would make them for you. They mourned the fact that their own children wouldn't celebrate *Bayram* in the same way. All they wanted to do was go away for a holiday. Skiing in the winter and somewhere by the beach in the summer. The women reluctantly admitted they couldn't force their children to celebrate in the old way, because it was now too difficult. Aysun's family came from Bursa and there they all lived a few streets away from one another. They could walk to each other's houses, but living in Istanbul, they were too far away from each other to casually drop by and see everyone.

Despite the change in the way *Şeker Bayramı* is celebrated, it still illustrates the importance of family. Even now, more than a decade after I talked with Aysun, in the days preceding the start of *Bayram* the television is loud with ads for impossibly large boxes of chocolates and store catalogues, bulging with a myriad of assorted selections, clog letterboxes. On television stubborn brothers weep wildly on one another's shoulders after the first taste of chocolate has worked its magic and brought them together, ending the feud that kept them apart for years. The next moment we see a very old woman living all alone.

Melancholy music flows and swells to a crescendo when we hear the doorbell ring. Painfully she hobbles to the door, dragging herself along on a walking frame. We see her arrive at the door only to hear the sound of a motorbike receding as it draws away. Our hearts break as we see her sitting alone and the screen fading to black before a well-known chocolate company exhorts us not to forget our loved ones during *Şeker Bayramı*.

Many older people in Turkey, like everywhere, bemoan the passing of tradition and fear that modernisation is changing society for the worse. In Istanbul, however, I still see evidence that customs and manners associated with the past still exist. On buses old people and pregnant women are never left standing, and in the supermarkets the young reach to the top shelves at the request of shrunken old women needing help. This helpfulness extends beyond respect for one's elders and is part of a more general desire to assist those in need.

A lot has changed since I listened to that impromptu concert in a dusty little stationery store in central Turkey. Literacy rates are higher, there are internet cafes in every other street even in the smallest of country towns, a lot more people speak English, and timetables are displayed at bus stops even if they are still sometimes little more than a suggestion. Yet despite a deep desire to be modern and to change, Turkey remains, in essence, Turkish. It is most noticeable in Istanbul, which historically has always been host or prisoner to people from other countries. No matter who has been through the gates of the city, *Istanbullu* Turks put people first, and never fail to take me by surprise with their sudden acts of kindness and generosity.

Whether it is the young girl on the bus giving up her seat because I don't look well and am none to steady on my feet, or the complete stranger who takes the piece of paper I am clutching and helps me find an elusive address, Turkish people connect to foreigners because many of them are themselves immigrants in their own land. All over the country Turks are united by the importance they place on human relationships and their sense of place but scratch away the surface and Turkey reveals itself as a complex society made up of a wealth of traditions and diverse cultures.

Made in the USA
Monee, IL
01 July 2022